Before Our Eyes

Lawrence Joseph

BEFORE

OUR

EYES

Farrar, Straus and Giroux

New York

Library of Congress Cataloging-in-Publication Data
Joseph, Lawrence.
Before our eyes / Lawrence Joseph. — 1st ed.
p.   cm.
I. Title.
PS3560.0775B44   1993   811'.54—dc20   93-9625 CIP

Grateful acknowledgments are made to the editors of Boulevard,
The Kenyon Review, Michigan Quarterly Review, Ontario Review,
Pequod, Ploughshares, *and* Verse, *where poems in this book*
originally appeared, some in earlier form. "Some Sort of Chronicler
I Am," which appeared first in The Kenyon Review, *also appears*
in The Best American Poetry 1992 *(Charles Scribner's Sons,*
1992). "Generation (After Akhmatova)" relies on Richard McKane's
translation of the "First" of Anna Akhmatova's "Northern Elegies,"
from Post-War Russian Poetry *(Harmondsworth, Middlesex,*
England: Penguin Books, 1974).

For my sister, Barbara,

and my brothers, Robert and Mark

Contents

Before Our Eyes

Before Our Eyes

The sky almost transparent, saturated
manganese blue. Windy and cold.
A yellow line beside a black line,
the chimney on the roof a yellow line
behind the mountain ash on Horatio.
A circular cut of pink flesh hanging
in the shop. Fish, flattened, copper,
heads chopped off. The point is to bring
depths to the surface, to elevate
sensuous experience into speech
and the social contract. Ribbons of smoke
silhouette the pier, a navy of yachts
pounded by the river's green waves.
By written I mean made, by made I mean felt;
concealed things, sweet sleep of colors.
So you will be, perhaps appropriately,
dismissed for it, a morality of seeing,
laying it on. Who among the idealists
won't sit in the private domain,
exchange culture with the moneymakers?
Here's one with acute hypertension
ready to crack the pressure cuff,
there's the type whose hallucinatory
devolution of the history of tribes
is personalized. My grandpa? He never
contended where Lebanon's history

began, if the child prince was smuggled
by his mother to a Catholic family
in the Mountain where he passed his boyhood
in his father's religion, a Druse,
the most secret sect of Islam.
I received the news in Jerusalem—
the Beirut Easter radio event, the dancer
undulating to sounds of explosions
outside the studio. The future isn't Africa,
my friend, and Europe's a peninsula of Asia,
and your America's a creation of Europe,
he laughed, the newspaperman, pointing
his finger. Still, don't street smarts
matter? Waiting rooms, shopping centers,
after all, empty moods and emotions.
And no denial's built up inside me.
It was, I admit, more charged than
I thought at the time. More predetermined.
Silver and red scraps inside the air,
cascades of sublimated pig iron.
Language more discursive, a more sequential
expression, and I attested to it.
The old dying? The new not yet born? The old,
the new, you fool, aphorized by Henry Ford
in '22. First make the cars, the roads
will follow. Modes of production created

of their own accord. The process runs
of its own accord. Current and diaphanous
sight and sound, comprehended, but poetry
I know something about. The act of forming
imagined language resisting humiliation.
Fading browns and reds, a maroon glow,
sadness and brightness, glorified.
Voices over charred embankments, smell
of fire and fat. The pure metamorphic
rush through with senses, just as you said
it would be. The soft, subtle twilight
only the bearer feels, broken into angles,
best kept to oneself. For the time being
let's just keep to what's before our eyes.

A Flake of Light Moved

Sunset, for a while
animated, colors appeared
out of nowhere.
We crossed Cornelia Street,
ate dinner in the open air.

"Love," she observed,
or was it me? I looked around.
Diagonal shadows slid across
one façade after another,
down to the river.

At the table opposite
a deeper blackness.
Something in the contour
of that ebony shape
caught my eye.

A flake of light moved. The great
island intermingling
watery lilac haze. Everyone
watched, as if hypnotized, and more,
much more, than that.

Material Facts

On the J train, a gun swung
toward the wide-eyed messenger
with a crippled hand, a burly man
wearing sunglasses tells
witnesses "be cool," the bullet
shattering a window after
ripping the heart apart.
At the Canal Street station,
slowly up the steps, head down,
he's vanished into Chinatown.

Rush hour. Chilled September
morning fresh and red clouds
beaten into purpled
bronze tarnished green. In front of me
another apocalypse is making
gestures, punching in and out,
hat askew on a conical head, ears
pointed like artichoke leaves.
Over there a boy scoots
a dog on a board with wheels.

I'm cool. Another double espresso
and a memory too, possessed
by finesse, a dissociated
sense of the voice of the stranger

who laughs the word "really"
out loud, his designer jacket
covered with zippers, flirting
hard with the woman employed
by the Caffè Giotto. Myself,
self-made, separated from myself,

who cares? That woman wears
a very tiny scripted name
on the chain around her neck.
Something about words and grief
I've forgotten. Something about
words and tears is forgotten.
Note that, on the new jail's wall,
the bas-relief of Confucius
comes off as decoration. See,
people want what you've got,

and, higher up, the visions
are clear: massive, dark blight,
millions with nothing to do;
ministers of every nation
courting financiers the way
the princes of Suzdal used to
kneel before the Golden Horde.
Regulators, assembled, argue

whether the freedom of speech
embraces government computers.

That's that. And this child looks
almost sideways at you,
suspicious, narrow blue face.
Then, grizzled in a tattered coat,
earflap hat and plaid pants,
a star of the screen, after a take,
switches into Popeye the Sailor,
an earlier role, entertaining
those behind the barricade
who laugh and applaud until

reality changes the script.
A child again, who doesn't use
words at all, says something
by slightly turning a corner
of the mouth, hiding material
facts from your perception,
standing beside a carp in a large
iron tank swimming upside down
in the window of Bank Central Asia
on a corner in Chinatown.

Admissions Against Interest

Taking my time, literal as I seemed, crazy
enough for silly disputes, actually Asiatically

sorry-eyed, reconciled finally
to the fact the January snow

behind the silver shed was only that,
the sudden sense you've seen it all before

appearing to take shape. For the likes of me
the weather wasn't any theory,

only conflagrations of the specks of a scene,
of rain the smell of smoldering soot,

clouds sweeping crimson down the street,
a physical thing. Bound by the Continual

Ministries of Thine Anger—a funny sight,
on both knees, all or nothing

outside in, wanting evil to disappear,
a complex character rattling off his complexity

the way, in Arabic, my grandmother would.
Mind you, though, my primary rule:

never use the word "I" unless you have to,
but sell it cheaply to survive.

II

Now, what type of animal asks after facts?
—so I'm a lawyer. Maybe charming,

direct yet as circumspect as any other lawyer
going on about concrete forces of civil

society substantially beyond anyone's grasp
and about money. Things like "you too

may be silenced the way powerful
corporations silence, contractually"

attract my attention. The issue's
bifurcated. "Why divide the dead?"

the Foreign Minister asks, "what's one life
when you've lost twenty million?"

And if what has happened during my life
had been otherwise could I say

I would have seen it much differently?
Authority? Out of deeper strata

illuminations. A lot of substance
chooses you. And it's no one's business

judging the secrets each of us needs:
I don't know what I'd do without my Double.

III

So the times demanded figuring out,
and on winter evenings beams of violet

appeared, thin and violent. Gorgeous violet
Avenue, gentle, frightened look. The state's agency

assigned to the task of measuring toxicological
effects on the sticky matter

of recollection cells doesn't have any idea.
The air roundabout the Bridge can't be

gold. "You know it makes you want to
shout," the girl on the bus, laughing, shouts,

throws both her hands up, the same song
tuned up on her radio, and I'm off into a mood again,

another internal swoon. So certain combinations
never before are worked on and hard,

knowing early on I could never act
as if I didn't think. My best cogitations

dwell in air so thick it weighs
on the skin, a solid complex, constrained

by this woman's clear fierce eyes wet
in this rain either with rain or with tears.

IV

And so I've had, vast and gray, the sky
my heart, amazed, determined by

the sight of a shimmering simulacrum,
undisturbed color. My admissions

against interest look smaller,
confirmations of another order.

My ancestors are on another plane,
never wholly innocent feeling any horror,

soul-contracted children of common cells,
never wholly distributed sensations

dejected into vertical visions and desire.
So I too am late at my singing,

too much to the point, but now I'm seeing
words are talk and words themselves

forms of feeling, rose-colored splashings
the ice-cold dawn, reliance upon

bare winds pouncing that dot of fire
inside compressed half-luminous air

deflected out of those places I see
formed into feeling, patches of light.

Under a Spell

Now the governor of the Federal Reserve Bank
doesn't know how much more he can take
while my thoughts wander outside me and can't be grasped—
I'm under a spell. While the prisoners
on Death Row whose brain cells will reach
the point of boiling water during electrocution
receive blessings through cable television
and Presidents and Commissars devise
international house-cleanings
history won't recognize for years,
the precedence of language and image preoccupies me too
under the influence of a spell.
Under a spell you have to remember
Monday morning of the insurrection,
the body in the ruins of Stanley's
Patent Medicine Store on John R
a block away from Joseph's Market,
when we argued time and space and memory are the same,
worked at The Rouge or The Axle,
read essays by an activist monk on non-violence
unaware of the strains we placed on our souls,
skies always choked by gray clouds
moving at different speeds, slag piled
pink and black at the end of the streets.
Under a spell paradise opens again,
a labyrinth. The vistas down the cross streets

are slabs of sun. The confused time
we cried in each other's arms.
Returning at the end of the suffering
to myself who loves no one. Returning
years later to that smoky twilight, still easy to find,
the breezes and sea smells from the Hudson
unexpectedly surrounding us, your eyes
unusually blue. Only you—with whom I can't pretend—
see everything go through me. Nothing's said
when you turn and look through me.

Over Darkening Gold

I

So here we are. Thieves stealing from thieves
in a society of complex spheres,
wondering what you should do. And still
stars blown outside the eye's corner.

II

The babies are asleep in beautiful lines.
But your eye's circuit is going so fast
we're no longer human. In that other place
a dog is still wailing in the background.

III

She said, "That's what I said." She said it.
"Desire isn't a form of sorrow," she said.
Around us wild metallic shimmering,
history, a subject, inside the sky.

IV

Inwards—and backwards, too. The difficult
memory of a divisive memory, killing
the order of the day. The state of the state
consumes the sublime ebony of the moon.

v

Ease up! No, ease down. You're right.
These days one must be especially careful.
The determined are constantly moving,
formed over gold, over darkening gold.

Generation

(after Akhmatova)

Matter smashed—Atomic Age America—
accelerated, dawn's desert light
blinding new. Kaiser Aluminum
spouting luminous brass vapors
at the bottom of the steaming valley.
Reality depends on (rumor has it
in The Café Society Downtown)
what you look at. Reality
in the woman's mind: her lover,
before he died, must have seen
a whole city quivering, blossoming
fire-bombs, pink and bright green.
It depends how you look at it,
phantasmagorical United States;
yet an astute observer perceives
melancholy anger on the faces
of illegal strikers resembles
looks of workers Diego Rivera
cartooned in his Detroit Industry
fresco of the thirties.
    Mildly opaque Indian summer sun
    a newly broken painted colt
    out of control scents alfalfa
    twisted by winds over land not yet
    disfigured by bankruptcy. Circling
    snow beyond a forested slope

from up above a whirlwind blows
horizontally against an ancient man
walking on ice to fill a house
of titmice with bread and water.
Optimism?—that would suppose
Miami ideas opposed to Chicago
facts; but vision sustains,
a style of seeing: a child catches
sunlight in a pocket mirror,
refracts it into a senator's eyes.
Of course, America contains its grand
gardens, lakes of roses, a monkey on a leash
chewing a pomegranate, glass after glass
of cocaine-pulque, orbits of fear.
Nerves sensitive to orbits of finance
are permitted to express what a girl
in a smelt furnace can't. I know that.
You do too. You know about the zigzagged
plutocratic brain, i.e., increased
incidence of schizophrenia (even back then)
right through the nation. You are too
struck by the state of flux, everything
natural, even the half-comic nature
of the suburbs, democratic views,
oil derricks in front of the State Capitol,
a pubescent boy with diamond molars,

banks named Manufacturers and Republic.
  Allurements, personalized sentiments,
  covenants restricting the sale
  of property to anyone descended
  from anyone born in Africa or Asia,
  hatred of the poor, hatred condensed.
  Goats under observation in Berkeley
  survived Bikini, statue of Jesus
  hands opened miraculously bleeding
  (and those dark deep liquid eyes
  of such color transposed dusk,
  hands strong and soft, wry,
  sad smile, frailty I could not know
  bequeathed by her, my legacy).
  Time, hypertense, turned into breadth
  —a piece of flesh is stuck to a shoe!—
  lightning syntax the color of skin
  soaring over undifferentiated
  difficulty and necessity: a pen's
  aqua ink on paper without lines . . .

So that's when we got the idea in our heads
to be born, not to let the sights
slip away, choosing in a badly measured time
human form over non-being.

Time Will Tell If So

A time of comedy sprung
to the eye, a sensational
time of substance and of form,
iridescent existences,
and the same old low-life.

Go ahead and laugh. Who
needs an imagination?
The thug with a wax complexion
guarantees his audience
you can have anybody killed for

a crate of imported oranges.
Circles of yellow mist
coiled from the open sea,
an old man approaches,
salutes, then walks away.

From one instant to another.
I can't keep my eyes
away from those fingers,
those beams of light
in the middle of the air.

An aura? Time will tell
if so. Alone at a window

lustrous with amber rain,
a figure, realized,
resonates, exhausted by love.

About This

I surfaced from my reflections to see
wartime. YOUR BANK ACCOUNT AND FUCKING COUNT

a sign on the mirror of Le Club Beirut,
an obvious object of interpretation during,

quote, the month that shook the world—
and here and in Paris the fashion news

this season color runs riot. Once again,
in the midst of delirium, my companions

on the subway, those who clean offices
all through the night, close their eyes,

Ash Wednesday-faced, much less anxious,
even more exhausted. That beauty's

green-gray eyes slanting like a cat's
must feel the battery of world views.

I do, and believe Nebuchadnezzar in his bunker
religiously is watching himself on Cable

Network News. Where's my sense of humor?
Prices are soaring in the futures pits.

There—over there are the Asian refugees
starting to tear apart the sewage pipes

under the villas to moisten their lips.
Here I squint into the twilight's blazes,

into stabs of dazzling dark radiations,
a set of sights attending my sun bath.

One of us, very old, stops uncontrollably
laughing, sighs, sighs, three, four times,

before starting in again. That rickety one
staring hard at the digital disc player

on display in the World Financial Center's
Palace of Palm Trees covets precision.

Gold (the old favorite in times of stress)
has relinquished its post-invasion gains.

Enough of a shooting war, military
expenditures, there may be no recession.

Is it true, the rumor that the new
instruments of equity are children, commodified?

That the Attorney General has bit off his tongue?
Those are—nails! that maniac wearing

wing tip shoes, turning a tattooed
cheek, throws at us while we talk about evil

outside, over burgundy, at the Cloisters.
This is August and September. This is wartime

bound to be, the social and money value
of human beings in this Republic clear

as can be in air gone pink and translucent
with high-flying clouds and white heat.

Whose Performance Am I Watching?

It's this way, by these words, too much yet still to be proven,
on the table in the café the soft laurel-like leaves,
stamens tinged yellow, outside, inside the winter
like a flash, sky thundered silver, outpourings cold
and distended, indistinguishable from a mood of the mind,
the time of sadness far away. "It's very nice," the father says
to his daughters, seizing a point of light out of the air,
drawing it out, looking hard at it, inhaling a cigarette,
opening and closing his eyes in rapid bursts of feeling.
"Just look!" and I did, and there, on the street, Hudson Street,
a rose-colored woman about to kiss a rose-colored man,
both of them older, under a linden tree, behind them
the elevated absence you've learned to let be. I've never
forgotten the expression on their faces, the only
human beings I've ever seen without that rapacious look
everyone else is possessed by. Brightness streaming in every
direction. Judgment, desire, sentence structure taking place.
Not in Siena, but right here, the spokes of the streets
                    suffused by color.
In a nearby bar the youths, including the victims, members,
                    Born to Kill gang,
involved in a fatal argument over a cellular phone,
                    a Malaysian woman.
There, nevertheless, may be more to the story, after all
                    the exalted rooms,

the Board of Directors, the future determined
               a long time ago.
Exactly how much one poet's thinking has influenced
               what's in the air
—a veteran of a foreign war is washing his hands
               with imaginary soap,
whistling the tune of the Contra War video. I enjoy
               a good laugh too
at the old comic business. But once again the lure is there,
               everything accepted
hits you in the eye. Illustrated magazines burning on
               the Brooklyn Bridge.
No peace nor lack of peace, only the haze of a form. It occurs
to me the girl in an overcoat sitting alone is listening to
herself, eyeing me with an uncertainty that isn't malevolent.
The dancer in the shiny leather jeans says Europe's more subtle.
I'm sorry, I know, it's a private matter, I wouldn't let go
until late at night, my thoughts absorbed ever since.
"No, it is"—the famous member of the international press
gang mocked—"the truth. First Islam, then the Chinese,
then what do you think?" There I am, out of my depth,
in a kind of fire-green, confusing the words you and I,
taken still by the physical silence of your hands. My God,
my God, whose performance am I watching? Wouldn't I
     have to
do it all anyway for the sake of the child turned blue?

The current mood also changing, whatever it is, opaquely
composed and overwrought attenuation moved through floating
planets of space, dusted by stars. This situation.
On St. Luke's Place the tree edges melting. You feel
the river's cold. The filtered sunlight insinuating opulence.

Sentimental Education

So no self-centered anarchism
was of use, too manic the sense
of economy, employment and inflation
curved. Detroit's achromatic
sky for a son of lower
middle class parents like me
glowed. My baptism by fire
in the ancient manner,
at my father's side in a burning city,
nothing sacramental about it.

Everything was—everything fast!
Strips of twilight shadow sheened
transparency and cast
a concisely stylized groove
you could count on
around the door to the dance.
War days conscientiously objected to,
the racial on me all the time,
I knew my place, you might say,
and white-hot ingots

in their molds, same time,
same place blue jays among the marigolds
held their own beside
the most terrible rage, tears wept

for no reason at all except
what might have been,
—my mother's tears, for instance.
She doesn't sleep well
in this climate
composed of pale tints.

But first, back to Henry Ford.
Of the world-famous Highland Park Plant
Otto Moog, the German engineer,
in 1923 proclaimed (Vladimir
Lenin thought so too): "No symphony
compares to the music hammering
through the colossal workplace"
—proof, so to speak,
that speech propels the purposes
by which it's been shaped.

But back, first, to Marvin Gaye,
during an interview in Brussels.
"Remember the Turbans?" he asks,
laughing at the memory. "Cats
sported silk headdresses, sang up
a storm. Had this one hit tune,
'Please Let Me Show You Around Myself,'
the lyrics comparing enclosed

empty space to an open heart
showed me to appreciate language."

Back to, because you want to,
Grand Boulevard, excessive sky
hot and indigo, poured out
onto Hendrie. Inside the store,
Grandpa lifts you into his arms,
small as a single summer Sunday,
a kind of memory trance truly
dark, deep and dark, steel dark,
not as pure, but almost as pure,
as pure unattainable light.

What now? The palette's red.
The beggars wear red in their hair.
Red's contained in the place's currency.
The distance sustained between
subject and object looks red.
History, increasingly ephemeral,
is red. The switches of the music are
red while you mark the beat,
consistent with your education,
without any inner dispute.

Out of the Blue

Not that we lacked experience.
We simply had no talent for murder.
And then it was November again.

The air brisk and cold, lights clicked
softly in a burnished glow.
A world with its own wild system of desires.

Yet somehow more fragile.
In a completely different place
from its syntax, in fact—far ahead of it.

And who could not be struck by the notion?
A Great Wheel, gold and gray,
out of the blue, burst in flame.

Taking the shape of the moment.
Disappearing
in a crevice in the sky.

Brooding

How could I foresee
looking back seven
centuries, one rose
in the crystal vase
in the room where
she stood before me,
legs slightly apart,
golden dusk all over us
when she insisted
not to go on talking
as if I was dreaming,
arguing the Summa
Theologica's proofs
that God is the love
she was brought up on,
she and I. Always
this point of departure
always, ceaselessly,
pushed toward
particulars of light
insistent emotions
sometimes abstracted
rarefied air.
Not at all fazed
that man on Grand Street
is yelling, "Eloi,

eloi, lama sabachthani,"
I've heard the words
before. Blocks away
substance dealers
finance insurance
companies, purchase
pension funds.
Russia, I see, once again
appearing in
our minds. A conversation
at a private reception
for the recent celebrity
intellectual
of the almost freed
state—"No one," he
laughs at my inquiry,
"reads Mayakovsky
anymore." But, decidedly,
more astute than
the anarcho-capitalist
lawyers he easily
convinces what lies
deep in his heart
—a bag of the softest
leather, with many
zippers, on his shoulder.

Perhaps he knows
how perfectly
he mimics a southern
Californian—"Paradise is
a fuck-dance
to the rhythms on video
of electronically
sexual dollars"
—while here I am feeling
sorry for him,
soul sickness
which has, like our own
strabismic know-how,
caused the species
dementia praecox
in the corners of various
Chancelleries;
with all due respect
the soul brother
hasn't yet entertained
certain elegantly
styled arrangements,
transmogrified servitudes
no one believes.
God, but who could
conceive it all?

Excessive cerulean
winds consecrated
green, feeling in
the back of the neck
a kind of mingling,
a nearness from far away,
and the finest flower
of the nation's
Executive branch,
frazzled and fatigued
before the press
under April showers
in Memphis, Tennessee,
wondering out loud,
"There's no way
I can explain how
I came to be here"
—quickly brushed
permanence around
further fact:
in Bose–Einstein physics
past and present
generate wave
functions on
consciousness equal
to a laser beam's time.

What you see,
not what you do,
what we say is absolutely
modern. What
do I see? A baby's
mysterious inability
to open his eyes.
What do I do?
Mysteriously
a month-old baby
can't open his eyes.

Variations on

Variations on a Theme

I

Winter dragged on. Established remnants
fell apart, displaced by chaos, by functions.
Take the renowned banker who's murmuring
the socialization of money has become
an abstract force and he's nervous.
In the background, out of the ground of being,
a resident of the Hill, in her tin hut
at the end of the Manhattan Bridge, insists
she possesses a Master's degree in English.

II

My friend the priest is studying Malcolm's
X, how Detroit Red decided to redesign
his sorrow—"the X a cross," he contends,
though none of it the gnosticism popularized
in certain circles. The way my friend
sees it, the species is undergoing
a cerebral mutation three distinct types
will survive: those who need to kill,
those who wait silently for transformation,
and those, the militants, seesawing
between the murderers and the victims.

III

Tell me about it! Molten copper
burned copper into an ethereal haze.
"My God," she added softly, "it seems
so terribly long ago." No, this afternoon,
I actually saw one of my peers
pour perfume over the body of a shadow.

IV

And that's the law. To bring to light
most hidden depths. The juror screaming
defendant's the devil staring at her
making her insane. The intense strain
phrasing the truth, the whole truth, nothing
but sentences, endless sentences.

V

I haven't forgotten. The way you converse
—to attend once more to words as words.
I mean it. Lips and skin remember, a voice
on the Avenue sensuous enough to touch.

VI

Gesticulating his head forward, poking
his baby finger, intonations arising
in a manner of speaking without agitation,
he says to her he doesn't understand
metempsychosis. In Walt Whitman's country,
pink and turquoise rhododendrons are
like porcelain after the rain, square,
dark-blinded windows behind her eyes,
hazel and hard, relenting at moments,
bound at the corners by minuscule lines.

VII

The war is a few days old. In the ever-blue
the sun continues its journey. You won't
kill their love of the actual. Let them go
conquer the world, march with Alexander:
there is Ur, the Chaldean city, a bronze
flake on a rock; there are millions, millions
plunged and numbed by dreams of blood.
It was then I had an attack of madness
—the eyewitness account the vanquished
appeared as if from a mirage of hot

oily smoke in search of someone
to surrender to—which almost made me smile.

VIII

What are you saying? This light is famous,
its sad, secret violet, and, this evening,
West and East Rivers turned into one.
To remember and imagine at the same time
—that was the month of June that year.
Within the intensity you showed me
both cloudiness and transparency can be painted.

In a Fit of My Own Vividness

In a fit, you might say, of my own vividness,
feeling January's crystal cold light,
a kind of—what's the precise phrase?—
bias on my part.
It's hard to throw off what you're subject to.
Examining it closely, the house in Royal Oak,
a mother's footsteps in the hallway, her body
shaking, space and time she won't realize
in incessant distress. You think about a thing
like that. The Palm Sunday procession
halfway through the century, Christ Resurrected
painted on our candles. Yellows on yellows.
Codes in effect. Limitless
marketplace assumed
transcendence. Something or other
tempted fate. So much for a family market
reduced to the poverty line
by a freeway. Time opaque and nullifying
perspective materialized. Those years my father
cut meat for the Great Atlantic & Pacific Tea Company
(knew to slice away the sinewy nerves) working
at the other store a few nights a week for his brother.
It was hot. There was smoke. It was hell.
Fire stuck together earth and sky, broken glass,
blood on the streets, berserk not only on Asian
battlefields, those events never transubstantiated

the shades disturbed. While the perpetrator raged
into spasms, the automatic shot off, the bullet
surfaced (after turning in the hospital bed my father
said, "There's lead in my ass"). Some thousand
sixteen-hour workdays before you're sublime.
Sorting out, at a minimum, the issue changes
and moods do too. Your mother worrying anyway,
her name whispered over and over again to herself
in the kitchen. The Medical Consultation Report:
"multi-infarct dementia, left and right hemispheres."
Don't you raise your voice! No—did you think so?—
not tears! This discord enacts no measure.

After All

The truth of knowing,
the absolute of feeling
—those were your
words—what we know.

A distance that never
gives way. The grandeur
this side of heaven
must be immense, after all.

And just as well to
keep still evening's
gray velvet ricocheted
across the street.

Some Sort of Chronicler I Am

Some sort of chronicler I am, mixing
emotional perceptions and digressions,

choler, melancholy, a sanguine view.
Through a transparent eye, the need, sometimes,

to see everything simultaneously
—strange need to confront everyone

with equal respect. Although the citizen
across the aisle on the Number Three

subway doesn't appreciate my respect.
Look at his eyes—both of them popping

from injections of essence of poppy;
listen to his voice bordering on a shrill.

His declaration: he's a victim of acquired
immune deficiency syndrome. His addiction

he acquired during the Indo-Chinese war.
Specified "underclass" by the Department of Labor

—he's underclass, all right: no class
if you're perpetually diseased and poor.

Named "blessed" by one of our Parnassians
known to make the egotistical sublime

—blessed, indeed; he's definitely blessed.
His wounds open, here, on the surface:

you might say he's shrieking his stigmata.
I know—you'd prefer I change the subject

(I know how to change the subject).
Battery Park's atmosphere changes

mists in which two children play and scratch
like a couple of kittens until the green

layers of light cover them completely,
a sense of anguished fulfillment arising

without me, beauty needled into awareness
without me, beauty always present in

what happened that instant her silhouette
moved across the wall, magnified sounds

her blouse made scraped against her skin
—workers, boarded storefronts, limousines

with tinted windows, windows with iron bars,
lace-patterned legs, someone without legs,

merged within the metathetical imagination
we're all part of, no matter how personal

we think we are. Has anyone considered
during the depression of 1921

Carlos Williams felt a physician's pain,
vowed to maintain the most compressed

expression of perceptions and ardors
—intrinsic, undulant, physical movement—

revealed in the speech he heard around him
(dynamization of emotions into imagined

form as a reality in itself).
Wallace Stevens—remember his work

covered high-risk losses—knowingly chose
during the bank closings of early '33

to suspend his grief between social planes
he'd transpose into thoughts, figures, colors

—you don't think he saw the woman beneath
golden clouds tortured by destitution,

fear too naked for her own shadow's shape?
In 1944, an Alsatian who composed

poems in French and in German, exiled
for fear of death in a state-created camp—

his eye structure, by law, defined as "Jewish"—
sensed the gist. Diagnosed with leukemia,

Yvan Goll gave the name Lackawanna
Manahatta to our metropolis—Manahatta

locked in Judgment's pregnant days, he sang,
Lackawanna of pregnant nights and sulphurous

pheasant mortality riddled with light
lying dormant in a shock of blond hair

half made of telephones, half made of tears.
The heavy changes of the light—I know.

Faint sliver of new moon and distant Mars
glow through to Lackawanna Manahatta.

Above a street in the lower Nineties
several leaves from an old ginkgo tree

twist through blackish red on golden air
outside a fashionable bistro where a man

with medals worn across a tailor-cut suit
chides a becoming woman half his age.

"From now on, my dear," he says with authority,
"from now on it's every man for himself."

Lines Imagined Translated

into a Foreign Language

And then the logic of war
    succeeded the night
the day bright lemon
    winter sky thinned
to cold peach
    no visible polestar
at the horizon's end
    the Sea of Samarra
outlined before us
    a breach of Asia Minor
incandescent before us
    —"These are the opening
rounds of this war"—
    Fire Specialists
anonymously delirious
    journalists on
the bridge of the *Wisconsin*
    bound by rules
mutating and returned
    into violence.
And I? Am I mad
    or maddened imagining
those who can't
    imagine this return
into violence? No
    tears, we hear,

no sense of terribleness
     or sorrow, nothing
only immense excitement
     when the attack
begins, blocks of light
     suddenly flattening
arc of laser-guided
     purple-tinged halos
around the open night.
     Every bomb seems to be
hitting. Explosions
     weirdly traced
lapis lazuli.
     Bridges still standing,
bridges over the Tigris
     River still there—
no action at all
     in the city.
Look at this! This is
     a flash of light
which seems—it seems
     to have come across
north to south close to
     the Al-Rasheed Hotel
before it goes—almost
     like a shooting star.

Or is it? This is
　　the imperium
emanating from the District.
　　He didn't want to go
into the Service,
　　his mother says,
but would help her out,
　　do better than the streets,
go to school. Although
　　you think you
could be distressed
　　by it, don't you? See
—those who proclaim
　　myths of predetermined
superiority. Remember
　　—the Sykes-Picot Agreement,
wasn't it? Nerve-racking
　　the evidence
widespread public
　　fragility and debt
overhanging inventory
　　and armaments—but for
the realities
　　the litanies seem only
to exhaust us. Rule
　　by extended clans,

circles of racketeering
   oligarchies abstracted
by—abstractions!
   Mesopotamia's imperial
eminence around 2250
   B.C. overlapping
Egypt's disintegrating
   unities the spectrum
through which events
   multiply and become
—hallucinations!
   Don't worry: the children
will define themselves
   by their age at the time
of this war. Meanings
   imagined into the types
of verbal progression
   a corporate economy
sustains, the language
   of direct expression
subverted by exhaustion,
   not a result
of diminished anguish
   but how it's imagined.
"Look," al-Fekaiki, member,
   Revolutionary Command

Ba'ath Party Rule
    '63, says again, waving
his fork over dinner
    in Paris, "Maybe he is
out of his mind or crazy
    or maybe he wants
to die a hero."
    "Play by the rules, though"
she who wears a diamond
    on her thumb is quoted
saying, "No one bombed
    ever forgets it."
By way of contrast, taxi
    drivers are demanding
up to six thousand
    dollars cash to ferry
outsiders into Jordan.
    This is different:
so delicate the Embassy
    refuses to acknowledge
it's happened. An infant
    in Haifa suffocated
resisting her parents'
    efforts to fasten
her gas mask. I waited
    up all night for it.

A weather front moved
    through the area. Skies
cleared partly today,
    clouds, copper blue
shaded clouds again Sunday
    into the early part
of next week. Repeat it
    one more time, I'll
figure out the meaning,
    then I don't want to
talk anymore.
    In London, the Foreign
Office disclosed
    a report Mr. Hussein's
wife and children
    traveled to Mauritania
aboard three or four
    stolen Kuwaiti
airliners recently painted
    the colors of Iraqi
Airways. In a dispatch
    from Abidjan,
Ivory Coast, Reuters
    says an aide
to Mauritanian President
    Ould Sidi Taya

officially dismissed
the report as "ridiculous."

Just That

So that's it? Just that? No dream.
A memory, and it happened
a while ago. On Grove Street
a sophora tree slightly swayed,
soul to soul in the plum-misted chill.

II

You wait and see. That language doesn't work
anymore, its century is over. It turns out
Joseph's Market is as free as the boy with one arm
kissing the tangerine my father gives him.
The entire place—upside down. Only money
and credit move around, part of the future.

III

So I take another look at my circles,
see them through an aphorism or two.
You do what you do, and do what you must.
There's refuge in observation.
And never expect to make hard cash from a poem.

IV

Actually, the whole night's slow
snow embodied the autoworks'
dull yellow grasses, embankments,
the sweepings. The noisy chains on
Jefferson Avenue, that steamship whistle
blowing beyond Belle Isle,
heaven, in its way, rained justice.
The city rioting seems to have remained
more than a portion of the brain.
The place continues, a state of flux,
opera neither tragic nor comic.

V

His finger jabbing like a revolver,
a talking head in a high-backed chair,
His Honor suddenly takes his glass eye out,
places it on the bench. The Public
Defender's case, he laughs, is a "mystical
allegation." He is, after all, a lawyer.
He can measure what a word means.
In a prison suit the accused smiles, too,
when a point is made in his favor.

VI

What time is it? There's a taxi on the way
downtown. Sulphurous yellow's hot sweet
rose, furious counterpoint, gentle anxiousness,
and words reveal it: gold-pink, sun-shot,
wave-cord, green-gathered. Say no more.
It's there. Except to plead you begin
again, as soon as possible, beautiful secrets,
part of my element, out of mind, in the flesh.

A Particular Examination

of Conscience

Awakened by your body, in the first place,
against mine, sweet and frenzied
skreekings and trillings of starlings
on the fire escape, and a rose sky.
Succumbed again to my gluttonous
appetite for the paper:
the front-page headline "Delusion,
Benign and Bizarre, Recognized As Common";
the rumor Chrysler and Allied-Signal
decided to purchase General Motors
publicly denied by the spokesman whose quip
"We're going to buy Greece, instead"
panicked the jittery market.
This morning, thoughts of long ago,
the Gare de l'Est, the last time I saw her,
she was leaving for Berlin and farther.
This morning remembered, the first time in years,
Saint Ignatius's rule:
nothing exists except through the senses
(amid poisons from Bayonne blown
over the harbor). Too much time this afternoon
spent plotting against my enemies.
Crisscrossing the Brooklyn–Queens expressway,
cool gusts broken into rapid spaces,
one of my sorrows suddenly eased.
Beside me a worker driving a Fury

appeared exhausted, plastic dice
wrapped around his rearview mirror,
above us on the Division Street overpass
a boy bowing, bowing and praying.
Late afternoon conversation with—
I told him he talks the way Seneca would.
Constantly comparing, meditative
yet impersonal style—a moralist.
Computerized systems reduce decisions
to make total war to instants;
absolute speed equals instantaneous
terror, though billions can't read
—I had to tell him to lower his voice.
Imagination split forever—one side
fear, the other hope; no one knows
how to decide, even within oneself.
On Worth Street at twilight delicate
silver light struck through my spine.
Before the courthouse on Centre Street
a barefoot woman danced in a circle.
By force of emotion, the entire day,
thresholds between us more than we know.
Which wounds transformed by which acts of will?
Not crying, not laughter, the howling
tonight on Water Street doubtlessly
contradicted, doubtlessly raving.

Movement in the Distance

Is Larger Up Close

Apart from that, the sun came around
the same time. A certain splendor emerged
illusory and frail, like a rainbow.
Around where we were standing everything
suffused apricot brightness. Even the man
alone in the Café Fledermaus, his table
covered by an old salmon-pink *Financial Times*,
feels he's metering his thoughts, gesturing
as if speaking. These curved lines,

so many images, but I suppose it's necessary to observe again
the rest of it split all over the place, one part
like money, forever within the daily routine, another,
mixing suavity, fragments of harmonic nuances
reflective at the same time abstract and grounded by the beat,
under the influence of connoisseurs of rhythm,
not afraid of being blue, brain on fire from time to time,
longing intensified to the point of—yes. I hear
you. Your absence more palpable than your presence.
And me? I'm often short of breath these days.
But, then, so are the philosophers, whose problems are
the politicians' now. For example, that man you've seen
on television, the head of state who bunches his nails
onto his lips, throwing them outward as if under
the pressure of some invisible bouquet magically forced
out of his mouth, clacking his tongue, proclaiming

the inevitability between Kazakhstan and the Sudan;
and there are many new Americas to discover.
I don't know about you, but it all goes through my skin.
Like the woman over there coughing into the pay phone.
Enlightenment? I've got mine, you've got yours—then what?
I know a prophet who possesses the power of thought
    transference,
addresses women mostly, recently seen carrying an olive
    branch.
But can't you see eventually we will be forced to acknowledge
countless children possess an alien language, face it,

      get down! The hype alone's no beautiful thing.
      What's sold: used shoes to those who prove
      indigency. Hot and spicy pork for the ego.
      Vodka for pleasure, votive candles to the Virgin.
      What's bought: this displaced child, hugging
      a kneeling woman, about to ascend into limbo.
      So you rampage within yourself—you think
      you should be thanked for it? In history's optic
      movement in the distance is larger up close.
      This is no proverb. Of course I remember
      that day—boundless happiness and joy.
      The leaves in the park deep, irascible mauve.
      The crippled unemployed drawing chalk figures
      on the Avenue. Precisely. Where we ought to be.

Now Evening Comes Fast

from the Sea

The East River looks as black
as the Brooklyn Bridge's shadow.

Thinking back—but those days
are over! A darkening green

conceals the Heights, quivering
twilight cold. I can't

be alone. And yet, somehow
or other, in spite,

or because of you transposed
in the treble of light

that lingers where the music
remains, a great and nuanced

diamond sheet projects itself
at the end of the street,

against the sky. So, still,
refracted into depths,

all beauty isn't underlined;
indignant and ironic

events blocked on top of one another,
dislocations debited

to anamorphosized tribes, city
drawn, caressed, into

circles—do you follow me?
Now evening comes fast from the sea.

Occident—Orient Express

East and west, converged expression,
analytical instincts, erupted harmonies:
all night a blind woman listens alone
to the radio. And in Tokyo Madame Lenine's
grandniece eats air-blown tuna
pungent as caviar. What do I mean?
Language means. And Jerusalem hangs
mystical in lavender sky
while outside Bethlehem the prophet Elijah's
seen entering a UFO.

Straining to catch the light again,
colorless light, bunches of violets,
a proud, shy woman silently sipping tea.
The process of logical association
you can't escape: the taxi driver
flashes his teeth, "It's in the eyes,
you have to break the other's eyes."
But if you love to hear a heartbeat
you won't sleep well alone. At noon
parts of the world are black with sun.

Or this rumor out of Lebanon:
Party of God regulars taught to kill
by Vietnam War veterans from Las Vegas.
The People's Republic programmatically

nullifies half its language.
The Isle of Dogs' rumor the Prime Minister's
capillaries are quickened
by daily doses of electricity
—reservoirs of the impulse
to work something out every place.

Or this: Moscow, coveting cash, visits Bonn.
Before the bust of Adenauer on the Rhine
a vista appears in the Chairman's mind:
a bright nation cleft with roses
swaying in yellow and flame.
"Where there's a will
there's a way," he assures his bankers
in English, almost singing;
a priapism of form
everyone present giggles at.

Against my heart I listen to you
all the time, all the time.
Against my brain, more visible than dream,
the present's elongations spread
blue behind the fragrant curves
pure abstractions blast through
a fragile mind in a flapping coat
descending the Memorial's steps

toward incalculable rays of sun
set perpendicular into the earth.